GOD MADE ME

Written by:
Debbie O'Brien

Illustrated by:
Emily Davis

Dedication

I would like to dedicate this book to my children and very creative grandchildren who have been such an inspiration to me. Morgan, Chelsea, Lindsey, Hailey, Eli, Lucy, Emmie, Macy, Logan and Sawyer; I love you all!

I also would like to thank my husband, Ken, who encouraged me to go for my dreams and has always supported my endeavors whatever they might be.

Please note: This is an interactive book. When reading it with your child, do the motions indicated in parenthesis on the various pages. For little ones who seem to be created to move and wiggle, these motions will involve them in an active way with the story.

Did you know that God made you?
He did!
He made every part of you.

Your teeth,
bones,
skin,
and hair.

He made you very special and He wants you to take care
of your body because He loves you.
Psalms 139 in our Bible tells about how special you are to God. It says,

God made me and He knows everything about me.
He knows when I get up in the morning
(Yawn and stretch)

And when I go to bed at night.
(Put head on hands as though sleeping)

He knows where I am when I'm hiding
(Cover eyes)
even when I'm completely out of sight.
(Cover eyes again)

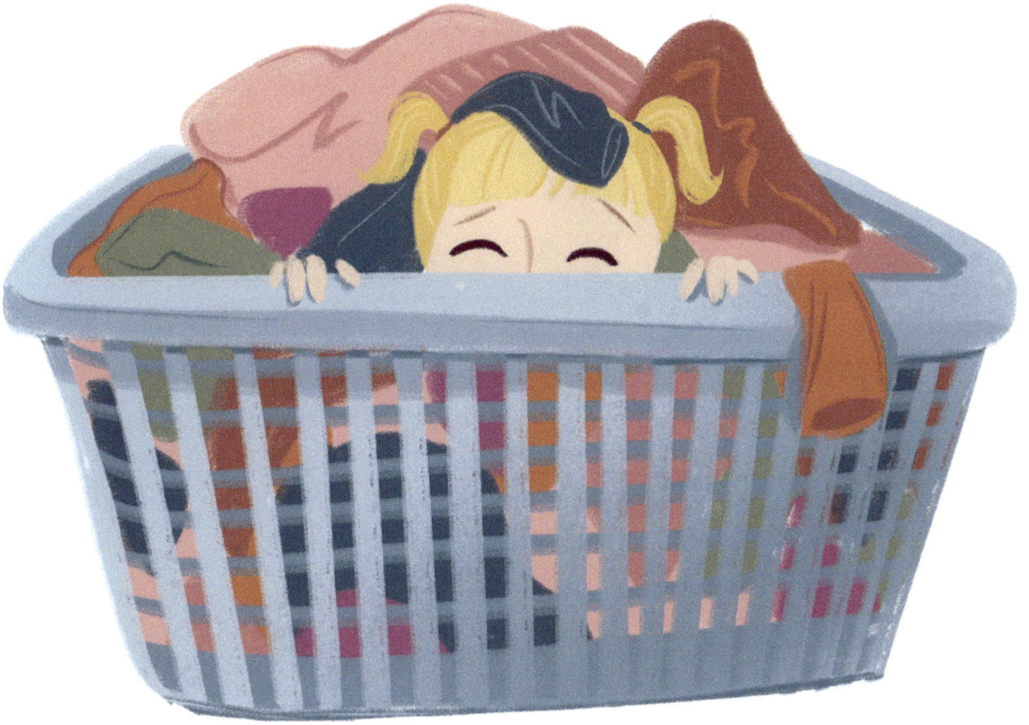

He knows what I'm thinking about and what I'm going to say.
(Hands by mouth)

He knows when I'm at home,

at school,

or at the park to play.
(Pretend to run)

He's never far away from me.
(Hands out to the sides then point to self)

Where I live, He knows.
(Put fingertips together above head like a roof)

Although I cannot see Him,
(Cover eyes again)
He's there wherever I go.

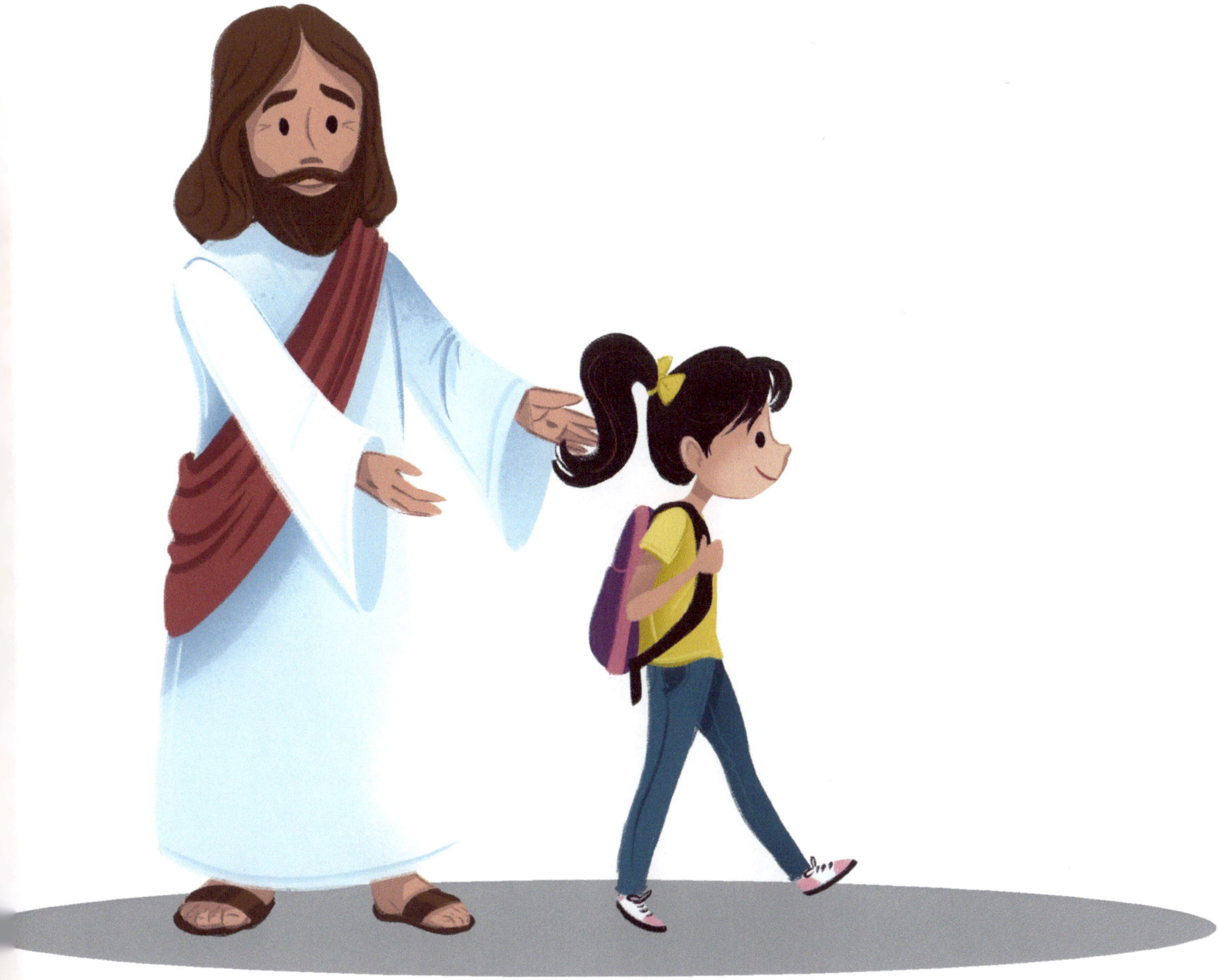

He thinks about me everyday, more thoughts than I can count.
(Count to 5)

Those thoughts add up to a magnificently, marvelous amount.

He created every part of me both inside and out.
(Point inward and then outward)
I am wonderfully made. It makes me want to shout!
(Shout, "Yeah God!")

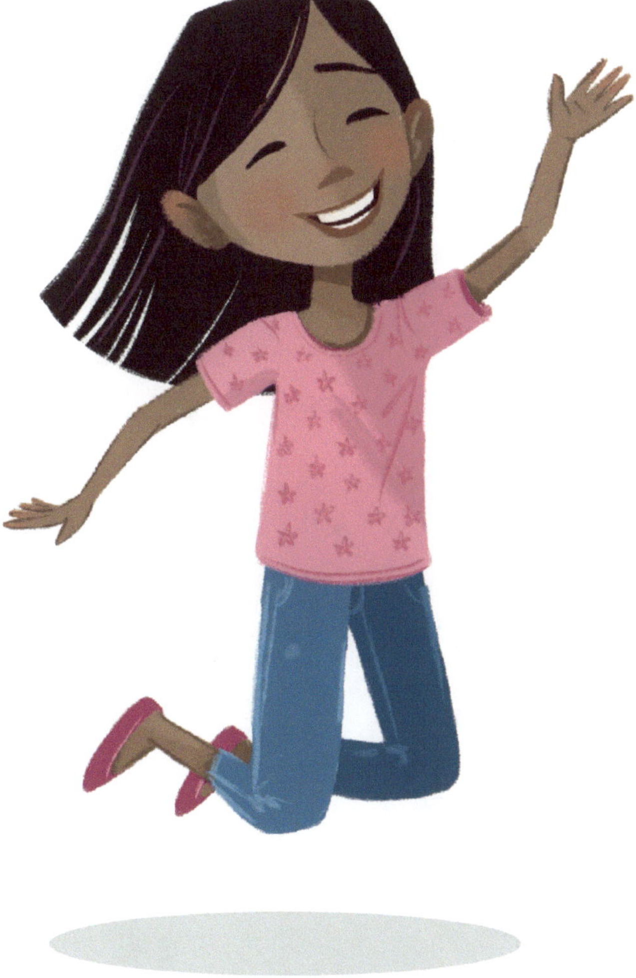

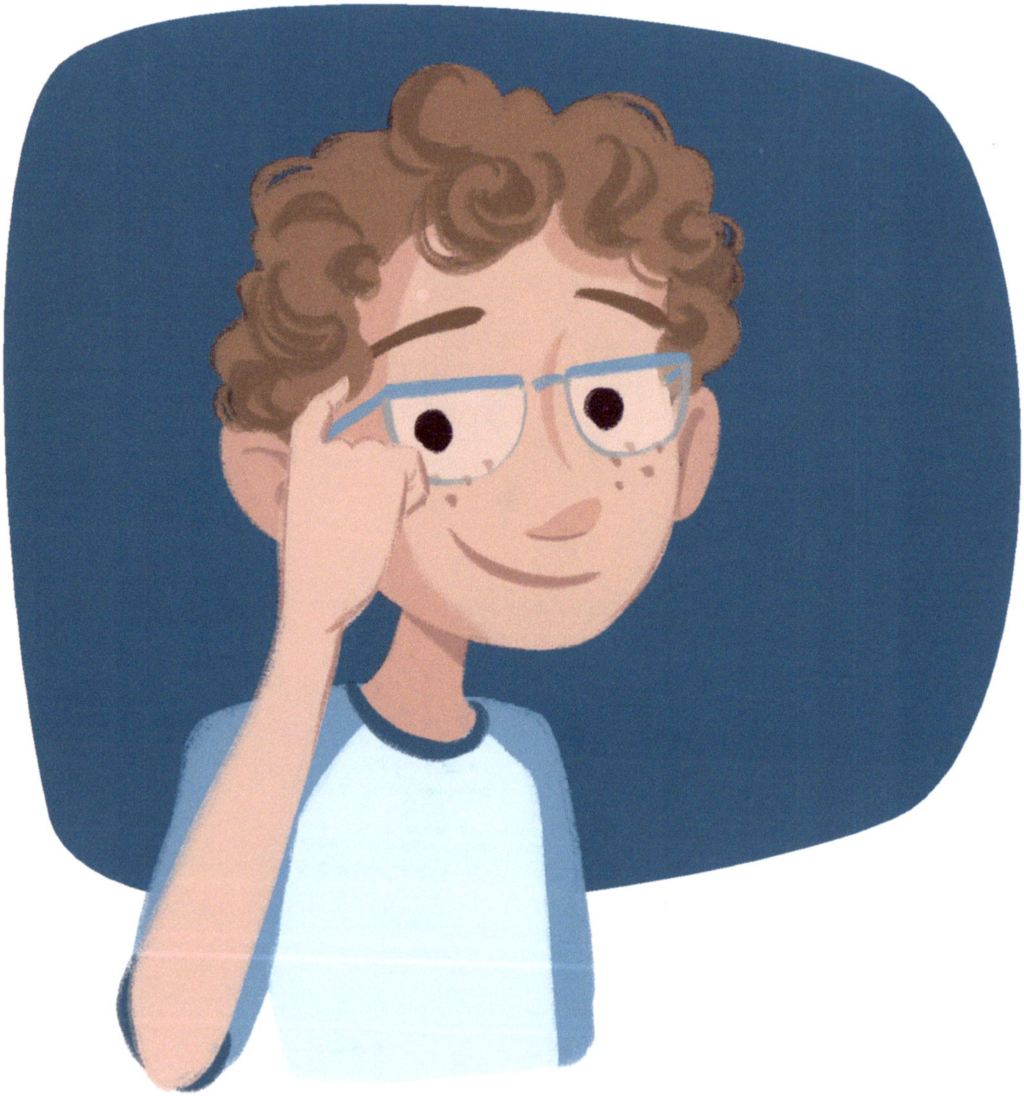

God, you're work is amazing! I know that very well.
(Fingers point to temples)
You have a special plan for me to live for you and tell;
(Hands by mouth)

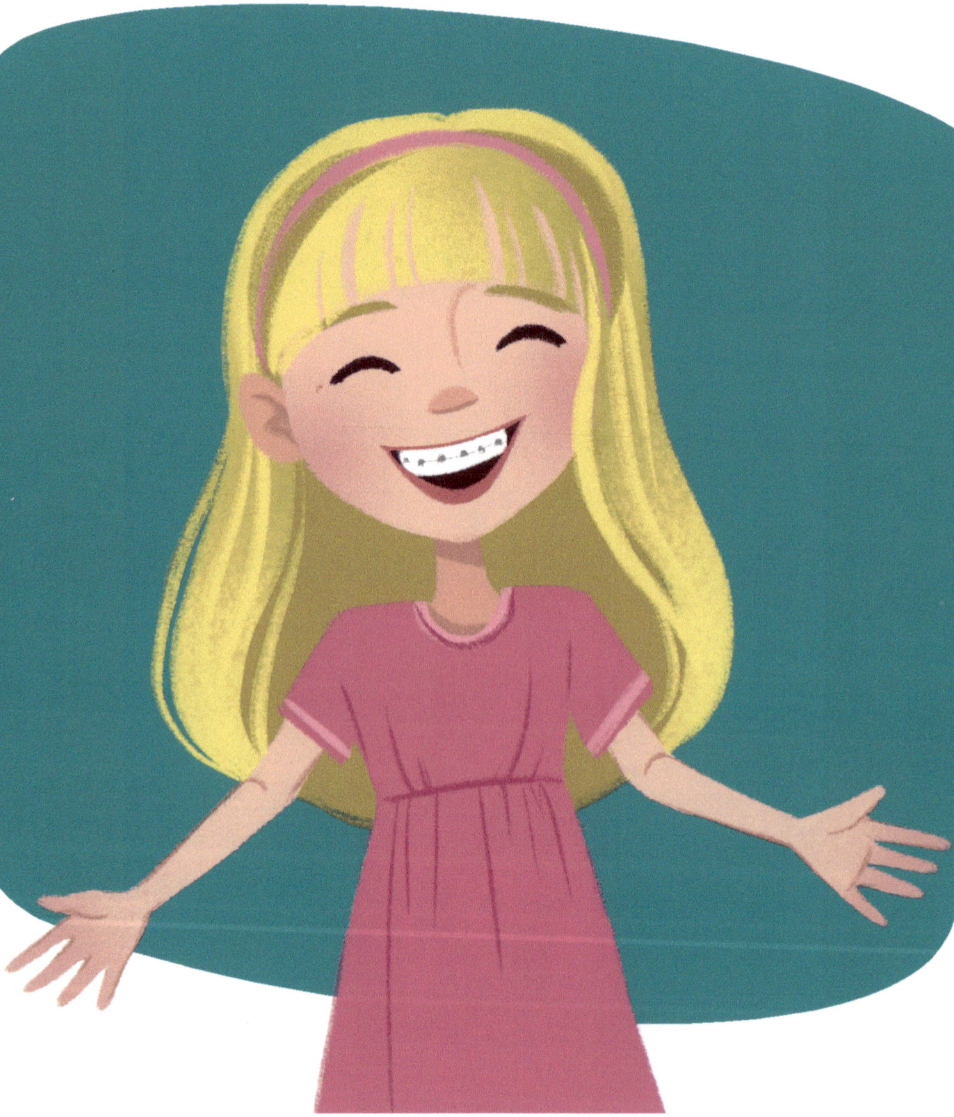

You know all I think and do, so help me to do what's right,
(Put fingers by temples then make fists and bump fists together)
I want to live for you, O God, morning, noon and night.
(Make sweeping, clockwise motion with hands)

Parent Prayer

Father God,

Thank you for this child you have entrusted into my care. Truly each child, each person is an amazing, one-of-a-kind masterpiece. Remind me, Lord, when I am weary, sleep-deprived and cleaning up yet another spill or wiping a runny nose or trying to lovingly discipline a wayward toddler, yes at those very times, give me strength; strength to parent with joy. Remind me of just how amazing (child's name) is and guide me to train in the way that You have designed. Give me teachable moments where we can learn together basking in your love and grace. Guide me to extend mercy and grace when such are desperately needed. When my child needs discipline and accountability, give me the strength to also give these with great love. My greatest desire is that (child's name) grows up to love you with all their heart. When the world is harsh or life threatens their worth, may my little one remember how wonderfully created, deeply loved, unique and special they are. Thank you God, for blessing me with this child. Amen